THE UNGUIDED TOUR

Isle of Wight

Simon Kern

❧❧

for Lucy

also
family, friends and acquaintances
past, present and future

Content Copyright © Simon Kern 2006
Design Copyright © Sixteen34 Ltd 2006

First Published in Great Britain 2006 by Sixteen34 Ltd

British Library Cataloguing-in-Publication Data
A Catalogue record for this title is available from the British Library
ISBN 1 84114 570 X
ISBN 978 1 84114 570 9

Distributed by: Halsgrove, Halsgrove House, Lower Moor Way, Tiverton, Devon. EX16 6SS
Telephone: 01884 243242   Fax: 01884 243325   Email: sales@halsgrove.com   Website: www.halsgrove.com

Printed and Bound by: D'Auria Industrie Grafiche Spa, Italy

Designed and Published by: Sixteen34 Ltd, Great Britain
www.Sixteen34.com

TIME MAY BE MEASURED BY ITS LENGTH
YET THE ISLAND REVEALS ITS DEPTH

THE
UNGUIDED TOUR

Isle of Wight

Simon Kern

❦

SANDRA DICKINSON

FOREWORD

In the early nineteen seventies I made my first visit to the Isle of Wight. I had arrived in England a few years before and knew nothing of the Island. A friend of mine generously offered to fly four of us there in his small private plane. Sick with the fear of flying in such a small plane but fascinated to see this new Island, off I flew. I hardly saw anything as I could barely open my eyes as we landed. My memories of this first sighting consist of a vision of a small deserted airstrip and a warm glass of lager and lime on a sunny day. One cold December day, some years ago, I met Simon over a bacon butty in the Sandbanks in Poole and we became firm friends. Simon is a native of the Isle of Wight. He invited me and my partner Mark to visit the Island for a guided tour. On this occasion I saw the Island through the eyes of a man in love. Simon knew everything about his homeland from its geological oddities to the nocturnal wanderings of its ghosts. He greeted me with a compilation of photographs that he had taken of the Island. He was afraid time would not permit my seeing everything so his photographic map would fill in any gaps in our tour. This map was stunning, a pictorial map in the shape of the Island made especially for me! It would later become the cover for this book. What I had once seen as a flat rather bleak landing strip was revealed to me to be an extraordinary, varied, breathtakingly beautiful, even magical isle. I suggested he make a book of the photographs for everyone to enjoy. Simon did make a book of the photographs, made and sewn entirely by hand. It was a work of art, an exquisite jewel like the Island itself. He has now had this book published for everyone to enjoy. Pick it up and let it seduce you, and you too will fall in love with the Isle of Wight.

BY

SANDRA DICKINSON

Isle of Wight

West Cowes
East Cowes
Porchfield
Wootton
Fishbourne
Newtown
Ryde
Havenstreet
Bembridge
Yarmouth
Calbourne
Newport
Arreton
Brading
The Needles
Sandown
Freshwater
Brook
Shorwell
Brighstone
Shanklin
Godshill
Chale
Ventnor
St. Catherines

It probably would not occur to someone living, say, in the middle of England, and some 70 miles from the sea, that they are living on an island. Therefore, what sets the Isle of Wight apart from the mainland is not just the surrounding sea, but the size of the Island itself, and our proximity to these naturally imposed boundaries. Whether it is the gate at the end of the garden, or the edge of our village, city or county, we spend our lives living within boundaries that make us feel at home. The Island offers us a comforting sense of community and place. If here long enough to begin exploring some of the Island's 147 square miles of nooks and crannies, one soon grows accustomed to just how big this 'compact and bijou' diamond really is! From the Needles on the western tip of the Island to Bembridge in the east is about 26 miles, and from Cowes in the North to St. Catherines in the South 13 miles. Between these four points the landscape is so varied: from downland to dell, farmland to forest, secluded bay to rocky outcrop. It is the Islanders themselves that shape the everyday Island, not only giving it life but also keeping it alive, just as they have for centuries. Less tangible, perhaps, is the spirit of this extraordinary Island. This is not to imply any particular notion, yet there is definitely something about this place that gets into the soul. It has inspired the creative minds of so many. It is a place of innovation, leisure and natural beauty as well as somewhere many are proud to call home. With an eye on the present through photographs and a glimpse of moments past through words, this book is intended to take the reader on a gentle, meandering journey around this fascinating and most beautiful Island. Although it may help to read the book in order, it is anticipated that the reader may also wish to dip in on occasional visits to this celebration of the Isle of Wight; to which they will always find themselves most welcome.

BY

SIMON KERN

CONTENTS

BOULDNOR

BOULDNOR

Millions of years ago major earth disturbances caused the once horizontal layers of sand and clay to dip and fold, leaving the strata we see in the cliff faces today running at various angles. But here, at Alum Bay, the strata have turned almost vertical, creating stunning seams of no less than twenty different coloured sands. The bay gets its name from the large deposits of alum discovered here during the 16th century, a chemical principally mined for tawing and dyeing hides. During the holiday season children can sometimes be heard to count the number of steps as they descend from the cliff top to the beach below, with the occasional pause to rescue their melting ice cream. Over 200 steps lead down the mouth of the chine, the Victorian path having long eroded. However, you may wish to arrive via the vertigo-enriching chair lift! Highly recommended, especially when you initially reach the edge of the 160ft. drop. The pebbled beach is flanked by the huge band of chalk cliffs which lead the eye out across the bay to captivating views of the Needles in the hazy distance.

ALUM BAY

Surely this must be one of the Island's most perfectly situated churches. Tucked away at the end of a steep sided lane just off the road to Chale Green, it is not until you have walked to the end of the lane and looked back over your shoulder that you discover this delightful sight. For there, nestling on the top of a small and unassuming hill, at the heart of the Island's smallest parish, is the church of St. James. Well trodden stone steps lead you up to the pleasantly proportioned graveyard, with its low boundary wall and numerous memorial stones. From here the church commands wonderful views of the surrounding fields and downland. The western corner of the graveyard reveals, lying close to the foot of the small hill, an impressive seventeenth century manor house to which this manorial church was once its chapel. Kingston Manor still retains some of the feel of its earlier medieval form from which it was hewn. Seen from the graveyard is the rear of the manor with its massive chimney stack and the gardens.

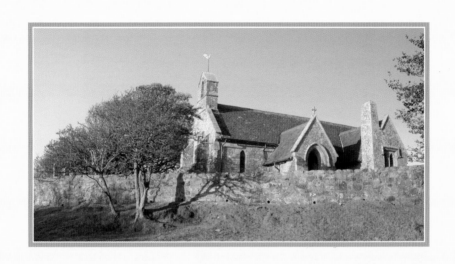

THE CHURCH OF ST. JAMES
KINGSTON

NEWTOWN

BOULDNOR

Scratchells Bay lies on the southern side of the Needles peninsular. Accessible only from the sea, those lucky enough to find themselves landing on its long narrow shingle beach, are presented with one of the Island's most exclusive picnic spots. Understood to have derived its name from one of the Devil's many nicknames, Scratchells Bay, like numerous other points around the Island's coast, has become the last resting place for ships foundered upon rocks lying just below the surface of the sea - rocks which are subsequently named after the doomed vessels. The St. Anthony went down here in 1691, and the Irex went down during a stormy night in 1890. Beneath the lowering chalk peninsular at the southern end of the bay, known as Sun Corner, is a large concaved arch. The distinctive angle of the flint banding adds a great deal to the beauty of these chalk cliffs. Above the bay is the old missile and space rocket test site. It was from here that in 1971 the only completely British satellite was launched into orbit via an all British rocket. The satellite is still up there, and set to orbit the Earth for at least another 200 years.

SCRATCHELLS BAY

Perched on the top of the 700 foot chalk cliffs of what is now known as Tennyson Down, above the foaming turquoise waters, rests this elegant Iona cross. It was raised as a memorial to the Poet Laureate, Alfred, Lord Tennyson, who lived with his wife Emily at Farringford House from 1853. At night, from the rooftops of Farringford, he would pursue his interest in astronomy. But by day, whilst striding out across the peaceful downland wearing his distinctive cape and wide brimmed hat, famous works such as 'Charge of the Light Brigade' would come to him. His poem 'Crossing the Bar' was written in his eightieth year whilst returning to Yarmouth from Lymington. The Tennysons played host to many illustrious Victorians, and pilgrims would head towards Freshwater hoping to catch a glimpse of the famous poet and his friends. Visible from miles around, the 38ft granite cross is inscribed: 'In memory of Alfred Lord Tennyson, this cross is raised as a beacon to sailors by the people of Freshwater and other friends in England and America'.

TENNYSON MONUMENT

Yarmouth is a town blessed with unspoilt charm and on bright sunny days it would seem to exude a quality of light quite unlike anywhere else on the Island. The all wooden pier is possibly the last remaining in Great Britain with its distinctive Victorian lattice railings and pier head supporting a small pavilion, originally the Pier Master's Office - useful these days if you get caught in the rain. Construction started in the summer of 1875 opening the following year at a total cost of £4,000, from a loan taking until the 1920's to pay off. Steamers calling at the head of the 650ft pier would not only ferry passengers to and from the mainland, but between other seaside towns on the Island itself. The journey by sea proved quicker and less arduous than by land. In recent times, with new timbers, hard work and the generosity of many people, Yarmouth's pier was given the opportunity of delighting Islanders and visitors alike for generations to come. Still today one can embark on a pleasure cruise, a spot of fishing or simply a gentle promenade.

YARMOUTH PIER

T H O R L E Y

WELLOW

Mottistone Manor resides within its beautiful terraced gardens beneath the ancient sweeping downland. The present eastern wing, on the right of this photograph, was built in the 15th Century on the site of a Saxon manor house, by Robert Cheke. His grandson, Thomas, added the western wing during the 16th Century. After his death it went to his cousin, John Cheke, who was the first Professor of Greek at Cambridge, and tutor to the future King Edward VI. Later he became Secretary of State and was thus knighted. On the 6th July 1553, aged 15, King Edward died of poisoning. Sir John's involvement in the plot to put Lady Jane Grey on the throne, instead of Mary, caused him to be sent to the 'Tower'. He died shortly after his release. In 1706 a huge landslide caused hundreds of tons of soil to fall from the hill behind the house to the height of the eaves across the rear of the eastern wing. It was not removed until over 200 years later, when General Jack Seely moved into the manor during the 1920's. Village harmony is completed by its picturesque church and green.

MOTTISTONE MANOR

BROOK BAY

BROOK

Many coastal towns are home to sailing clubs. Their history began with the predecessor of the Royal Yacht Squadron in 1815 which gained its Royal patronage in 1833. It was not long before a number of other clubs were founded, some also gaining Royal approval. With clubs like the Island Sailing Club, founded in 1889, and before that Bembridge, accepting a less elitist membership, the sport of sailing became even more popular. The most spectacular event in the sailing calendar must be the Island Sailing Club's 'Round the Island Race', held every summer since 1931. About fifteen hundred yachts of all types take part and when the spinnaker is unfurled, so too is a sea of colour. Landlubbers follow the intrepid by car or bicycle or for brief stretches do all they can to keep up on foot. Some, however, take advantage of a vantage such as Gore Cliff, where they remain with binoculars, sea air and picnic, from the first hazy sighting of the leading yachts rounding the Needles, through to those with the less competitive prerequisite of just a fun day out!

THE
'ROUND THE ISLAND RACE'

The presence of Queen Victoria living on the Isle of Wight had such a profound effect on its development that it would be difficult to imagine its evolution had she not chosen to make the Island her home. Victoria and Albert built Osborne as their Island retreat, where they could be free from the pressures of London life. Her influence was such that she unwittingly, although with no detriment to the tranquility of Osborne, turned the Island into one of the most fashionable resorts in the country. When, in September 1846, the Pavilion wing was completed, the family moved into their new home. 1851 saw the completion of the main wing and with this, the workmen and their families were treated to an open-air dinner and dance. Albert, who had designed the Italianate styled house, continued by directing the landscaping using semaphore from the top of the flag tower. Victoria had remarked how she enjoyed the blossom scented air drifting in through her sitting room window, whilst listening to the nightingales sing, and watching the moonlight shining on the sea.

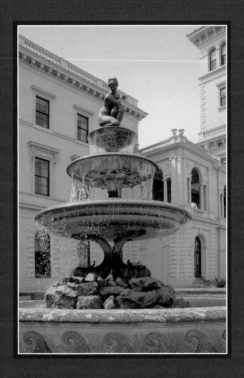

OSBORNE HOUSE

Victoria and Albert had nine children, for whom the Swiss Cottage chalet was built in the grounds of Osborne. Here, along with play, they were encouraged to learn such things as gardening, carpentry and cooking. Occasionally the Queen and the Prince would be invited, by the children, to dine at the cottage. The happiness the family shared was changed forever with the death of Albert in 1861. Victoria retreated to her seaside home, and withdrew from public activity for almost a decade. Queen Victoria became Empress of India in 1876 which was later reflected at Osborne in the additional Durbar wing. Princess Beatrice married Henry of Battenberg at Whippingham Church in July 1885. Two years later the Island celebrated their Queen's Golden Jubilee and in 1897 her Diamond Jubilee, with street banners such as: "Good Sovereign - no change required". Victoria died at her beloved Osborne on 22nd January 1901. Still to this day Queen Victoria draws visitors from all over the world to what was once an Island close to the heart of the Victorian era.

OSBORNE ESTATE

Heavy waves have undercut the base of these cliffs, the recession of which has left behind a platform of chalk. The extraordinary beauty of this is only revealed at low tide, when long furrows ploughed by time and tide form this field of chalk, which appears to gently incline some 75 feet out towards the grasping sea. Limpets cling to the ridges patiently waiting for the returning tide, whilst tiny crabs are blessed with shallow, elongated pools of water left by the previous tide. Above, the gulls and cormorants lap the 300 foot chalk cliffs of the Island's eastern promontory. These 80 million year old cliffs of chalk are made up from the fossilised remains of billions of tiny marine plants and creatures. Although this all looks very serene in the weak afternoon sunlight and with a calm sea below, the tides are quick to turn and, together with the precarious terrain and even the occasional falling rocks, it is not without its dangers. Sheltered from westerly breezes, Whitecliff Bay itself, with its broad sandy beach, is an ideal spot for a game of rounders!

WHITECLIFF

Today perhaps Totland is more popular with locals, for long gone are the pleasure steamers that made this one of the busiest resorts on the Island. Once brimming with day trippers, bathing machines and boats, Totland boasted one of the largest hotels on the Island. During the late 1850's three brothers from neighbouring Colwell Bay were given the job of shipping the huge granite blocks for use in building the Needles lighthouse from Portland to Totland Bay, whereupon they were hewn into shape. After this they then had the perilous task of getting the blocks out to the Needles. Despite the fact that Freshwater has long since encroached on Totland's boundaries, the village's individuality sings out with its use of locally produced red bricks and red tiles covering roofs of all pitches, including triumphal towers and turrets, some with finials. This plethora of red contrasts wonderfully with numerous mature trees. Perhaps one day Totland's pier may once again overflow with holiday makers enjoying the summer regattas.

TOTLAND BAY

In 1893 fifty acres of land were acquired on the parish boundary, just north of Gatcombe withy beds, for the proposed Whitecroft Hospital: the county asylum for the mentally ill. The architect was Mr. B.S. Jacobs of the East Riding and the builders were the London firm of Garlick & Horton. Six large two storey blocks were required to house over 300 patients of various mental infirmities. In turn, kitchens, a laundry, a mortuary and farm buildings would be required as well as staff accommodation. Somewhere in the region of three million red bricks were used in the hospital's construction, all of which were made to order on site, whilst stone was shipped over from Swanage. Happily perhaps, for most people Whitecroft has only ever been the closest landmark to the centre of the Island. With its two clock faces, the glorious campanile water tower, which houses a bell weighing half a ton, can be seen from some considerable distance throughout the surrounding hills and valleys. The tower remains one of the Island's most impressive landmarks.

WHITECROFT

Springing from downland areas, the Island's rivers and streams meander towards the sea, sometimes seen, sometimes unseen, occasionally only heard. Those heading for the back of the Wight suddenly encounter the sheer cliff edges of this coastline which have, over time, eroded the soft clays to form deep gullies or ravines known as chines. Most of the Island's twenty chines, each with a character all of its own, are found along the back of the Island, a number of which provide the only access to local beaches. Evidence has found early communities living around chines providing water and food, and shelter for their boats. Nowadays the clifftops are honeycombed with rabbit warrens, akin to luxury homes with sea views. Wind and tide dissect this ragged coastline allowing us to see millions of years into the past. This has made the Isle of Wight one of the best places in the world for finding dinosaur remains: some of which were discovered here first. As springs dry up or streams are diverted chines are born or reshaped. They are indeed one of the Island's most awe inspiring natural features.

WHALE CHINE · CHALE CHINE · LADDER CHINE

From the broad sweep of the Bowcombe valley to the snug seclusion of a fluttering canopy of green, and its wonderful wooden footbridge, is how the village of Shorwell greets its visitors. An engraved stone on the eastern embankment beside the bridge tells us 'This foot bridge was reconstructed in 1976 by public subscription and voluntary labour. The original bridge was built in the 18th century.' A walk across the rustic bridge leads to shady dells of trees young and old. The name Shorwell is said to derive from the Anglo-Saxon, meaning 'the spring rising from beneath a steep hill'. This spring still rises up from within the beautiful grounds of Northcourt Manor and adds to the charm of the village inn, as it flows through the garden and beyond to the sea, via Grange Chine. It once powered Yafford Mill which lies further southwest of the village. Northcourt, with its light grey stone and pinnacled gables, is one of the largest manor houses on the Island. Shorwell is steeped in a rich tranquility, with picturesque cottages and a lovely church, all nestling beneath the downs.

SHORWELL SHUTE

For some, the Devil's Chimney serves as a momentary respite from the heat of a summer's day. A steep flight of uneven steps in a narrow cleft of the rockface either leads the weary up to a cup of tea, and the stunning views above the canopy of trees, or down into this enchanting bower known simply as 'The Landslip' (as if it were the only one to have occurred on this Island!). Lying between Luccombe and Bonchurch, this tangled haven of trees, moss, ivy and fern cling to acres of land which, during major landslips occurring in 1810 and again in 1928, was sent plunging ever closer to sea level; in this case Steel Bay. A myriad of little paths venture among the rock and root strewn undergrowth. Eventually the dappled light may take you past the wishing seat or further on to Luccombe, or, with glimpses of sea on your left occasionally bearing a yacht, into the idyllic village of Bonchurch. Here, Victorian villas bask on stone clad terraces and among pretty gardens, all beneath the highest point on the Island, St. Boniface Down.

DEVIL'S CHIMNEY

One of the most rewarding ways in which to approach Seaview is to walk in via the coast. If you venture from as far away as the neighbouring town of Ryde then you may choose to vary your journey by way of the woods at Appley, and across the top of Puckpool Battery, or along the sea wall parallel to the arc of gabled beach huts; and then perhaps along the beach at Springvale. But, from whichever direction you approach Seaview, one is always greeted by its nostalgic charm. Once it boasted an elegant five span suspension pier; sadly lost during a storm one night in December 1951. Seaview started life as a quiet fishing village and today is a nautical retreat; with lively coloured dinghies sleeping against the sea wall and locally built wooden dinghies gently bobbing on their moorings. Seaview is simply buzzing with life during the summer months, as both Islanders and visitors gather along the sea wall soaking up their pints and ice creams, along with a little news from abroad, whilst the children play amongst the rock pools below.

SEAVIEW

Adjoining the old deer parks, half a mile from Appuldurcombe House, is the estate's northern entrance, the Freemantle Gate. Being almost isolated from one of its original purposes, that of an entrance or exit, makes the Freemantle Gate one of the Islands most magnificent follies. If its other purpose was to make a statement, well then it certainly achieves that aim. The triumphal arch, of the Ionic order, was built around about 1774, some 73 years after Appuldurcombe House itself was begun. For about 300 years this Queen Anne house, in the architectural style known as English Baroque, was home to the eminently well connected Worsley family. The grounds were landscaped by Lancelot 'Capability' Brown. Sometime during 1943 a landmine exploded near the house, damaging the roof and windows and accelerating the house's dilapidated state. 1986 saw the replacement of the roofs and windows in the three east facing rooms. The Freemantle Gate never ceases to impress, and to find it for the first time by chance alone, is pure serendipity.

FREEMANTLE GATE

A S H E Y

EAST ASHEY

Once upon a time steam locomotives could be seen puffing through this rural tranquility. These days it's only walkers and cyclists! Most of the Island's railway network has been converted into foot & cycle-paths or, in the case of a tunnel, a home for mushrooms and bats! However, the track between Wootton, Havenstreet and Smallbrook requires less imagination. Here, beneath plumes of grey, regular trains roll by, nostalgically invoking a bond of friendship amongst strangers, as onlookers and passengers of all ages empathically wave at one another. A sight that gladdens the heart. The railway arrived on the Island in 1862, serving Cowes and Newport. Over the next 28 years, owned by no less than five companies, it grew to well over thirty stations and halts, encompassing most of the Island's major towns and villages. Much of the railway's rolling stock has been second-hand, including today's electric trains which are 'ex-underground'. In return for this, and its isolation from other networks, the Island's railway has gained a charismatic life all of its own.

SOUTHFORD

Surrounded by broad vistas of serenity, the pinnacled silhouette of St. Mildred's church beckons without the need for bells. Numerous churches have appeared on this site but the latest incarnation was designed and built for Queen Victoria and her family by her husband, Prince Albert, and the architect, Mr. A. Humbert, who went on to design Sandringham. Dedicated to an Anglo-Saxon Princess who became a nun, this splendid church begins its individuality at the top with its five pinnacled square tower which houses an octagonal lantern. Then there are the rose windows, copies of those in Notre Dame Cathedral. The font was designed by Princess Louise. An airy opulence surrounds a plethora of memorials to the royal family. Princess Beatrice was laid to rest with her husband in a large marble sarcophagus. In the churchyard can be found the graves of Prince Louis of Battenberg and Princess Victoria of Hesse, who were the grandparents of HRH Prince Phillip. Part of the carpet in the church was used during Queen Elizabeth II's Coronation.

THE CHURCH OF ST. MILDRED
WHIPPINGHAM

High above the treacherous waters of Chale Bay, on the summit of St. Catherines Hill, stands what is locally known as the 'Pepper Pot': despite looking more like a medieval rocket! St. Catherine's Oratory is the only medieval lighthouse in Britain, making it the second oldest lighthouse in the country: the other being of the Roman period. According to folklore, in 1323 landowner Walter de Godeton had received some 50 casks of looted wine belonging to a religious order, from a ship run aground on Atherfield Ledge. For this he was ordered to pay back the cost of the wine and as penance build a lighthouse with an attached chantry from which a priest, who would keep the octagonal lantern lit, would say prayers for souls lost at sea. In 1785 another light, christened the Salt Cellar, was begun nearby, and not long after abandoned when it was realised the lights were too often shrouded in mist and fog rendering them invisible. If you need an incentive for climbing up the hill then try the spectacular views, and if you need an incentive to climb back down, try a tub of ice cream!

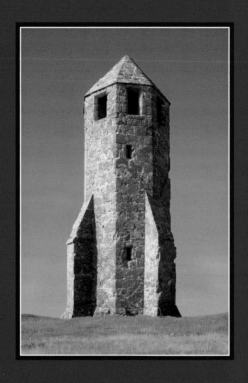

ST. CATHERINE'S ORATORY

Excise Duty ironically created the 18th century Islander's most worthwhile occupation - smuggling. A man spent his day a breadwinner, but by night most were tobacco, wine and wool-winners! The contraband was hidden in caves or chines, or disguised as rocks, until it was safe to distribute inland. Shipwrecks afforded extra bounty, yet if the wreck had already been spotted by customs then smugglers were in extra danger of capture. It was not until the spring of 1840 that another light began to shine over the 'Bay of Death', where most of the Island's 4000 recorded wrecks have occurred. This time round, the lighthouse was erected on the lower southern tip of the Island. But, just like its predecessors on the downs above, this modern light, even at its low altitude, also fell foul of thick fogs and sea mists. As a consequence, in 1875 its height was considerably reduced to that of 86ft. The light has a range of 17 miles, and its mournful foghorn was considered to be the loudest in the world - contributing to fewer wrecks and less smuggling!

ST. CATHERINE'S POINT

B O N C H U R C H

STEEPHILL COVE

The Parish Church of St. Lawrence was built in 1876 by Sir George Gilbert Scott, best known for London's Albert Memorial. The church's most striking feature would have to be the stained glass windows. In 1969, with the support of H.M. the Queen Mother, Lord Mountbatten and Sir John Betjeman, among many others, the glass was saved from the chapel of the demolished Royal National Hospital which dominated the site now occupied by Ventnor's Botanic Gardens. The window in this photo depicts St. Peter, one of two windows designed by the Pre-Raphaelite artist Sir Edward Burne-Jones. There is Ford Madox Brown's St. Luke and two by William Morris. Sir William Reynolds-Stephens' west window, depicting a physician treating the sick, is in the vivid style of Art Nouveau. It was the Victorian physicians who noticed this area's unique microclimate, considering it ideally suited to the treatment of people with respiratory diseases, such as tuberculosis, that led to the 1869 Royal National Hospital.

ST. LAWRENCE
PARISH CHURCH

Many of the Island's forests are worked for their crop of timbers and the large Brighstone Forest is no exception. Although coppicing still takes place today on a smaller scale, in the past hazel was coppiced for use in making hurdles and chestnut for fencing. Today these woodlands are home to a great many creatures, including red squirrels, for which the Island is one of their last remaining habitats in the country. Also dormice, the green woodpecker and butterflies such as the Brimstone and White Admiral thrive here. Rather than catching the eye, the abundant White Ransoms flower is more likely to catch the nose first, with the aroma of its common name, Wild Garlic. A number of wild flowers would seem to be unique to the Island. In the spring, the woodlands are carpeted with bluebells, and later in the year there is nothing quite like a walk through the golden hues of an autumnal wood, enriched by the incandescence of the low sun. Emerging from Brighstone Forest affords breathtaking views across the ancient downland to the coast beyond.

BRIGHSTONE FOREST

BEMBRIDGE

FORELAND FIELDS

Dedicated to the Patron Saint of England, St. George's Church, residing at the western end of Arreton valley, retains a unique atmosphere from its proximity to a thousand years of rural life. Belonging to King Alfred, the manor of Arreton eventually passed on to the Abbey of Quarr. Towards the end of the 13th Century a squat west tower was added which, in about 1480 was subsequently heightened to what we see here, along with its two massive buttresses. With the addition of a tower set against the original medieval west wall, a chamfered channel was included in the tower itself to allow light in from two existing lancet windows. The belfry has 6 bells, the earliest of which dates from 1559 and the youngest 1951. Within the sanctuary floor lies the headless brass figure of Harry Hawles who fought at the battle of Agincourt in 1415. Outside, west of the Elizabethan porch, is the red brick tomb of Oliver Cromwell's grandson, William, and his wife Martha. St. George's gains much character from its proportions and even more from its ancient setting.

THE CHURCH OF ST. GEORGE
ARRETON

Together with its mellow stone and beautiful proportions, Arreton Manor is probably one of the Island's most charming homes. This Jacobean manor sits in the fertile valley at the western end of Arreton's ribboning village. The present building was built between 1596 and 1612 with the addition of a central porch wing in 1639. During the 17th Century it was owned by three families: the Benets, the Culpeppers and the Fairfaxes, whose descendents continued to own the manor up until the end of the First World War. Some of the rooms still retain the original oak panelling, and above the fireplace in the dining room is an ornately carved overmantel bearing the Benet's coat-of-arms. The original manor on this site had yielded an extensive crop for its 12th Century owners, the monks of Quarr, to whom the manor had been gifted by the Lord of the Isle of Wight, Baldwin de Redvers. Still to this day the valley remains at the horticultural centre of the Island, protected by the downland to the north.

ARRETON MANOR

Carisbrooke Castle was begun early in the 12th century and takes the form of a motte-and-bailey (mound-and-enclosure) structure. The 'motte', crowned by its keep, which is reached by 71 steps, dominates the north east corner of the castle walls. As you would expect, the vantages from the ramparts are fascinating and spectacular. The drum towered gatehouse replaced an earlier square tower in 1335. Both towers have cross slots through which arrows could be fired and in the upper sections are possibly the earliest known gunloops of their type. Carisbrooke has defended the realm on numerous occasions due not only to the location of the castle itself, but to the proximity of the Island with the coast of England. It has also protected the Island's many lords and governors who have resided within its palatial halls, including Princess Beatrice, who succeeded her husband as governor in 1896. She was the last to use the castle as her residence, during the summers, until her death in 1944. Just as the castle has prevented people getting in, it has also prevented them from getting out!

CARISBROOKE CASTLE

In November 1647 King Charles I arrived on the Island seeking safety from his enemies under the protection of the Governor, Colonel Hammond. At first he had the freedom of the Island, through which he would drive visiting royalist friends. He was later confined to Carisbrooke Castle after a secret treaty with the Scots was revealed. In March, with everything arranged on the outside, he made what would be the first of two attempts at escape. Climbing out of his chamber window he realised, on becoming stuck, that the bars were closer together than first anticipated, and was forced to abort the attempt. In May, having procured nitric acid with which he loosened the bars, he tried again, but decided to remain where he was when he saw an inordinate number of people waiting for him below. Eventually he was taken for execution in Whitehall on 30th January 1649. In August 1650 two of Charles' children were imprisoned at Carisbrooke. In September the delicate 14 yr. old Elizabeth died of pneumonia and was buried in St. Thomas', Newport. Her brother Henry was freed in 1653.

CARISBROOKE CASTLE

Stumbling over the serpentine roots of ancient trees and bobbing under hefty trunks that have taken to growing almost horizontal, is all part of the charm and character of the narrow ravine leading up past Mottistone Manor. The great storm which swept through the Island, opened up this once darkly bowered path from which one eventually emerges to find, standing there before them, the Longstone. This Neolithic monument, which dates to about 4500 years old, marks an ancient long barrow at the western head of the valley above Mottistone. To the Saxons it was known as the moot stone, or 'the stone of the speakers', as it was used as a meeting place where discussions took place and decisions were made, most of which would probably have some legal point of view regarding land or live stock. Nowadays, much of the land around here is given up to growing commercial timber. The atmosphere across these parts feel different from other areas of the Island. It feels 'old'; but perhaps that's just the Longstone working its magic!

THE LONGSTONE

Wolverton Manor is one of three great houses to be built around the village of Shorwell during the more prosperous years following the Spanish Armada, late in the reign of Elizabeth I. It is in her honour that Wolverton, among others, dedicated the traditional 'E' shaped groundplan. The central porch is reputed to have come from the original moated house whose foundations are just to the north of the present house. Up close the colourful ferruginous sandstone implies a gentler side to Wolverton's imposing edifice, but its moods are at the whims of the weather. During the 18th century the back of the manor gained an extension intended to carry a staircase up past the fashionable addition of a Venetian window. Somehow the staircase never appeared, and the tall chamber never quite saw the light of day with the window remaining bricked-up. At one time, divided by two owners, the western half gained sash windows. Despite this cruel lack of symmetry, Wolverton hasn't lost its power to dominate its situation.

WOLVERTON MANOR

BROOK

BROOK

Consisting of about a dozen houses, many having been the homes of farm workers, the hamlet of Hulverstone, which lies between Brook and Mottistone has grown over many hundreds of years out of affiliation with the local farm. The Sun Inn has served the people of Hulverstone, Brook and Mottistone for nigh on 250 years. Yet this wonderful stone and thatch building may be almost twice as old. During the late eighteen hundreds Charles Seely of Brook Hill House, who played a large part in the creation of the Island library service, converted a local barn into a school. At one time there also existed a post office, both have since been turned into private homes. The Sun Inn almost fell foul of becoming a private dwelling some years ago but, luckily saved from this fate, it remains at the heart of this great little hamlet offering, as the blackboard says, food every day with curry night on Tuesdays. With our ability to traverse the Island with greater ease these days it may well be the popular 'local' to those living in the furthest reaches of the Island.

THE SUN INN
HULVERSTONE

CHILLERTON

CHILLERTON DOWN

Once the capital of the Island, Newtown is a village with the feel of a simple hamlet, although for a while it was a lively medieval town. The oldest of the Island's boroughs was laid out on a grid pattern, some of its medieval streets are now broad grassy tracks leading down to the quay. Its situation among tidal creeks and marshes is one of extraordinary beauty. Newtown's prosperity never fully recovered after it was raided by the French in 1377. By the 17th century larger trading vessels could no longer approach its quay as the sheltered harbour gradually began to silt-up. Oyster beds soon appeared, but it was the salt industry that flourished here until the early twentieth century. Newtown could so easily have disappeared altogether along with villagers forced to leave their homes to find work elsewhere. Today Newtown estuary, stretching out beneath the expansive skies, is a nature reserve, home to thousands of migrating birds. Apart from things like its isolated 18th century town hall, Newtown's tranquility would almost have us believing nothing had ever happened here.

NEWTOWN QUAY

The most notable feature to be found in the hamlet of Yafford would have to be its eighteenth century water mill. Built with an overshot wheel, it once took advantage of the fast flowing stream that eventually reaches the sea at the bottom of Grange Chine. Yafford itself is best described as a farming community with no discernable village. For many years the mill was a popular attraction open to visitors. But for now it has reverted to a private dwelling. With the strong growth in both naval and merchant shipping came the need for provisions such as ship's biscuits, and so the Island's mills found themselves in ever increasing demand. Well worth seeing is the earlier water mill at Calbourne; still turning as the Caul Bourne, from which the village gets its name, flows over the 20ft water wheel, heading for Shalfleet Lake and Newtown River in the north. Calbourne Mill, its fire station and outbuildings are home to a large collection of old farming equipment, and the farming equipment home to peacocks, ducks, and doves who find the nooks and mill streams the ideal idyll for the idle!

YAFFORD MILL

COMPTON

YAFFORD MILL

Opposite St. Mildreds Church in Whippingham is a row of terracotta red Almshouses whose mellowed vibrancy resides in harmonious contrast with its verdant surroundings. It was under the orders of Queen Victoria that in 1880 the Almshouses were built as homes for Royal servants who had since retired. The two chimneys of Kingston power station grab the attention of those looking north towards East Cowes. This is an incredibly atmospheric town, very sedate in comparison to its western counterpart. Here the streets are broad 'Sunday' avenues, lined with trees and rows of Victorian villas and terraced houses. Backing onto the Jubilee Recreation Ground is the elegantly proportioned Frank James Hospital. The opulent East Cowes Castle, home of the architect John Nash once stood on the hill now occupied by a housing estate, and sequestered among trees on the point is the 1799 Norris Castle. The seafront has seen the birth of flyingboats, the very first hovercraft and many ships. But the greatest form of transport, available to everyone, has to be the Floating Bridge!

THE ALMSHOUSES
WHIPPINGHAM

BEMBRIDGE

COMBLEY GREAT WOOD

In essence the Island has always been watermill country, and not for a lack of sea breezes has there only ever been a handful of windmills built here, and of these Bembridge is the last in existence. The mill is built from local limestone with its southern face protected from the elements with a layer of Roman cement. Its working life began during the early 18th century producing flour, meal and cattle feed. To position the thirty foot sweeps into the wind, the miller would rotate the cap from the ground outside the mill. By pulling an endless chain that hung over a wheel in the cap, a worm wheel would in turn rotate the cap into position. Inside, steep ladders climb the three floors, along with the central oak trunk driving the knarred array of wooden gearing, and the all important grind stone. Towards the end of the 19th century it was only producing feed, and by the autumn of 1913 it ceased work altogether. During the First World War it became a shelter for the Volunteer Reserve's night watch. During the Second it became a lookout and headquarters of the Home Guard.

BEMBRIDGE WINDMILL

C H A L E

IDLECOMBE

N A N S E N   H I L L

THE CHURCH OF ST. BARNABAS
BLACKWATER

The 'Village' gained its quaint 'Old' adjective when, during the Victorian era, Shanklin began to grow from here. The 350 year old Crab Inn, seen here to the left of the photo, was built at the top of Shanklin Chine, a deep ravine in the 100ft cliffs. Here, spring water pours over the 45ft falls and along the verdant chine where tall trees and rare plants thrive. Towards the end of the last war it was not only water that passed through the chine. A pipeline was laid under the Solent to Thorness Bay on the north of the Island, then across to Shanklin Chine via a pumping station. It was from here that over 50,000 gallons of fuel oil a day was pumped beneath the English Channel to the Allied forces in France. The green pipeline is still visible running along the base of the Chine. Despite Shanklin's growth, the town retains an air of Victorian romanticism. Shanklin station is where the twenty minute railway journey from Ryde pier head terminates. It was the arrival of the railway in 1864 that really turned Shanklin into the resort it is today.

SHANKLIN OLD VILLAGE

1892 saw the introduction of a lift to enable people easier access between East Cliff parade and the Esplanade below. Prices started at 1d per person and rose to 3d if you travelled with your bathchair and attendant. The Victorian lift has since been replaced with a more modern edifice. Shanklin lost its pier in the great storm of October 1987 and it seems unlikely to ever be replaced. Towards the northern end of the Esplanade is an amusement arcade which began its life as an old World War I seaplane hanger in Bembridge Harbour. During the early 1920s it was dismantled and moved to be re-erected in its present location, on Shanklin seafront, where it became one of the Island's premiere theatres. Many well known stars of the day would perform during the theatre's summer season. World War II brought about its end as a theatre when it was used to store the pipes for PLUTO – 'PipeLine Under The Ocean'. During the summer months the three wide sandy beaches are brimming with stripy deck chairs and their occupants.

SHANKLIN
CLOCK TOWER

The romantic sounding 'Knighton Gorges', often pronounced as K[ay] – nighton to distinguish it from the other Niton, refers not to the landscape, but the beautiful Elizabethan manor that once stood below the downs, perched above an ornamental lake. 12th century owner, Hugh de Morville, was one of the four murderers of the Archbishop of Canterbury, Thomas Becket. By marriage the manor came into the possession of the de Gorges, hence the name, and by the 1560s the Dillingtons. The last owner of Knighton Gorges, George Bisset, who entertained people such as the artist Joshua Reynolds, eloped with the wife of the Island's Captain. The scandal caused their ruin leaving Bisset a broken man. Later he forbade his daughter, of a later marriage, from marrying her cousin on pain of banishment. They did marry and in 1821 the dying Bisset ordered the manor pulled down. Only the gate posts and a few ghosts remain. Knighton Gorges has a reputation for being haunted; but then so does the entire Island, and why not? Where better to spend eternity?!

KNIGHTON GORGES

Those serving under the protection of 'Motor Gunboat 320' during the 1940s could hardly have imagined that sixty years later this vanguard of luck would have survived to become a floating hotel! The first houseboat, a retired lifeboat, appeared on the Embankment during the Edwardian era, and by the 1920s many other houseboats had arrived as holiday homes, some having originally served in the war. In the past Bembridge was virtually an island in itself with flooded marshland to the south, and from the north the River Yar, a tidal creek, stretching round to Brading Quay, making it an important haven for ships. At one time referred to as Binbridge Isle, with a causeway running out from Yarbridge, the name Bembridge is derived from 'a place within bridge'. Although by 1882 Brading Quay was inaccessible to larger ships, an embankment carrying the railway to Bembridge made Brading the inland town we see today. Opposite the thriving harbour, with its boat building, sailing and fishing, the lagoons are home to many birds.

BEMBRIDGE HARBOUR

Often the first you see of Quarr Abbey is its capped bell tower peeking just above the surrounding canopy of trees, and offering just a hint of its impressiveness. The Abbey is home to a community of Benedictine monks. Originally from Solesmes, they first resided on the Island at Appuldurcombe whilst Quarr was being built. Designed by one of the monks, construction began in 1908 and was finished by 1912 when it was consecrated. The Abbey, which lies just west of a ruined 12th century abbey, where Princess Cecily, second daughter of Edward IV, is buried, derives its name from the local limestone quarries which provided stone for buildings such as Winchester Cathedral. During the dissolution of the monasteries, stone from the medieval abbey was reused in the construction of the Island's Tudor fortification. To some, Quarr Abbey's angular nature may seem at first a little austere, and yet, the warmth of its Flemish brick will challenge the grimmest of weathers. The Abbey resides looking sublimely youthful amongst its mature grounds.

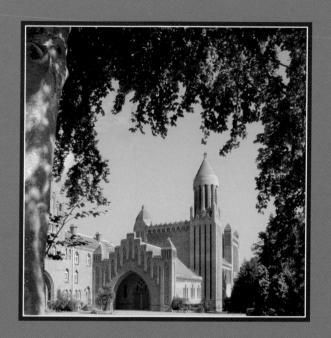

QUARR ABBEY

Restricted by its surrounding marshland and rivers, thankfully the medieval town of Yarmouth has never outgrown its narrow lanes and small shops. Yarmouth, like Newtown and Newport, were planned towns meaning they didn't grow sporadically through the influence of individuals. The town hall was rebuilt in 1763 and sits so comfortably among the square's fellow buildings as to almost allow it to go unnoticed. In 1668 Sir Robert Holmes became Governor of the Isle of Wight. Whilst moving up the Naval ranks to eventually become Admiral, numerous campaigns, including some dubious ones, made him a wealthy man. Charles II stayed with him at his home in Yarmouth on a few occasions; now the George Hotel. On one occasion Holmes had captured a ship carrying a marble statue of Louis XIV, and its sculptor, bound for France to sculpt the kings head from life. Holmes ordered the sculptor to sculpt his head on the torso as his eventual memorial. Today his statue stands proud in St. James church as a reminder of this remarkable character.

THE TOWN HALL
YARMOUTH

Fine villas lodge among mature gardens along one of the Island's finest thoroughfares. The lush and peaceful Undercliff Drive winds between St. Lawrence and Niton where many landslips have shaped the treacherous beauty of this area. Old Park House was once owned by Walt Disney's uncle, Sir John Cheape, before it was bought in 1882 by the German philanthropist, William Spindler. He began creating a garden village within the Undercliff. Trees and roads hidden among tousled Undercliff and storm strewn boulders in the bay, once the promenade wall, are all that remains. He also helped his neighbour, Mrs. Pearl Craigie, a novelist and playwrite under the nom-de-plum of John Oliver Hobbes, restyle St. Lawrence Lodge during the early 1900's, more commonly known today as Craigie Lodge. The Lodge was designed by a local architect and built in 1889. Nearby, the old parish church was once the smallest in the country, until, when in 1842, a chancel was added. This quaint little church is so obviously blessed with the love and care of its parishioners.

CRAIGIE LODGE

The pointy end of the Isle of Wight breaks away in the form of three huge chalk stacks, and rising from the outermost is the Needles Lighthouse. Its three foot thick wall stands on a chalk platform carved away with the aid of dynamite in 1859. Storms have sent waves crashing through open windows over halfway up the granite tower, and sometimes keepers were unable to receive supplies for almost a fortnight. The early nineties saw the end of an era with the automation of the lighthouse. The last keepers left their remote dwelling in December 1994. From 1897, Marconi's wireless experiments emanated from converted rooms in the Needles Hotel. Broadcasting over increasing distances, the first transmission was from one end of the billiard table to the other! But it was not long before messages were received by ships 40 miles out. The Needles headland is covered by the Victorian battery, with a tunnel out to the searchlight position on the point, and a lift shaft sunk to an emplacement close to sea level. The Needles are indeed the perfect ending to a great island...

THE NEEDLES

C U L V E R

INDEX